Praise for IMPACT & The Accidental Marketer Series

- IMPACT taught me the importance of understanding industry shifts in decision-making power, and of getting to true customer values vs benefits. As a result, we repositioned a product from an emphasis on "improved speed of procedure" to the more emotional "my surgical partner has confidence in me to do my part." With IMPACT's help, my team and I were able to transform our approach to the market and expand market share and market adoption. I also was able to take IMPACT's tools and techniques to other teams & companies and make an immediate impact there as well. **Jennifer Paradise,** *Former Managing Director & VP at Getinge; Marketing Lead at Ethicon*

- I love how these chapters are helpful in altering a business plan mid-stream (or in steady state). This book is an excellent tool kit to any marketers regardless of their tenure. When you are in the throes of trying to market a brand, there are times where you are so busy you have blinders on, or you forget about the 'little' things that play a big influence. **Cortney Dominianni-Smith,** *Executive Director, Commercial Effectiveness, Global Pharma Company*

- Not just an entertaining read peppered with lots of marketing stories but full of practical tools that can help form your strategy based on marketing principles. **Bryan Siow,** *Head of Corporate and Business Development at Elessent; Former Head of Strategy and Marketing at Halliburton*

- Impact's tools and expert moderation had a lasting impact on our business. Not only were we able to build a clear, strong strategy in days that could have taken months on our own – the tools and ways of thinking were timeless. The iterations of our plans for years after the engagement were much easier because the original strategy was so robust. And we saw the difference in our business results right away. **Jane Fuller,** *Founder of Fuller Insight LLC, formerly of Colgate-Palmolive, The Coca-Cola Company and Pfizer*

- It was like I was back in the classroom with IM-PACT – the stories are concise and interesting, and I still use the tools such as the Vietnam Card Sort. I really like the interactive components and how you lure readers to the podcasts and videos! **Ralph Elwell,** *Learning Leader, Energy Programs at GE Vernova*

[Click here](#) or use the QR code below to see more Impact testimonials.

The **Accidental** Marketer

CASE BOOK

Unravelling the Mysteries of MARKETING SUCCESS

Mary Abbazia
Tom Spitale
Sean Welham

Published by: Impact Planning Group, LLC, 90 Grove Street, Suite 206, Ridgefield, CT 06877
Copyright © 2024 by Impact Planning Group & the authors
Permission for use of downloadable strategy tools and podcasts:

Manufactured in the United States of America

Authors: Mary Abbazia, Tom Spitale, Sean Welham
    Title: The Accidental Marketer Case Book:
    Unravelling the Mysteries of Marketing Success
    Paperback ISBN: 9798218339395
    eBook ISBN: 9798218339401

Cover designed by Sean Welham
Author's URL: https://theaccidentalmarketer.com/

Contents

Why This Book Matters To You

As we connect with clients, whether tracing back to our early days or exploring future collaborations, we often find them sharing their well-worn copies (with post-it notes and scribbles) of our inaugural work, *The Accidental Marketer*. We are delighted, of course, but lately, we've consistently heard the same question: "Do these principles and tools still work?" The answer is "yes", but it's not as obvious as we all would hope (nothing worthwhile is!). With so much changing in business, we felt compelled to write this book to provide a roadmap to modern marketing success.

In an era where AI and technology continue to revolutionize industries, professionals with technical backgrounds are increasingly finding themselves in traditional marketing roles. These *"Accidental Marketers"* are looking to quickly gain an understanding of how to develop effective marketing strategies. *The Accidental Marketer Case Book* is the most practical guide available to help inexperienced marketers become proficient quickly.

This new *Case Book* builds upon the solid foundation laid by *The Accidental Marketer* and our extensive experiences with insightful clients. Delving even deeper, we tackle ten of today's most pressing marketing questions, spanning contemporary issues such as co-opetition, digital chokepoints (think the 'Uber-ization' of industries), and the rise of B2B content marketing. Each question unfolds across the ten chapters, using real-world cases that, while predominantly B2C, are designed to be relatable and effortlessly applicable to B2B scenarios.

Brimming with innovative ideas, each chapter highlights strategy tools that can be immediately applied to replicate the success of spotlighted companies. Free access to these tools is provided at the end of each chapter through QR codes and URLs. These tools can be applied independently or used together to build a strategy.

Our *Accidental Marketer Case Book* draws on practical concepts and tools refined in strategy sessions globally over the past 40 years. From executive programs at esteemed institutions like Columbia University and the California Institute of Technology (Caltech) to private engagements through our consulting firm, Impact Planning Group, we've empowered tens of thousands of marketers to glean customer insights, create differentiated strategies, and execute initiatives with precision. We have enjoyed learning from them and their experiences.

Crafted from our never-ending quest to uncover the drivers of marketing success in the real world, this new *Case Book* is your guide to differentiating your products and services…and winning. Whether you're a returning fan from *The Accidental Marketer* or just discovering our work, consider this book both a mirror and a window-reflecting timeless truths and offering fresh perspectives.

Cheers,

Mary, Tom, and Sean

Features of This Book

This book includes several interactive features that will enhance learning and the integration of the content into your day-to-day business. These features include:

- QR codes (for the printed version of the book) and URLs (for readers of the digital version) for easy access to materials.

- 13 downloadable tools that follow the chapter content and will allow you to adapt the strategies featured in the cases to your own business challenges. The tools can be used independently — or together to create a strategy.

- 10 podcasts that provide additional background and insight on each of the cases.

- An instructional video (The Vietnam Card Sort) that will show you how to have deeper, richer dialogue with customers and uncover needs they likely haven't shared with competitors.

We hope that these features will enhance your enjoyment and overall experience of reading this book!

Chapter 1.
How Do You Master Market Agility?

Featured Case: Kraft Heinz and The Case of the One-Way Mirror

Tool: Trend Analysis

Key Takeaways:

- **After three years of stagnant sales, packaged food corporation Kraft Heinz reported a loss of $12.6 billion and watched its stock tumble by over 20%. The titan's fatal flaw? Failing to respond to consumers' desires for fresh food.**

- **Internal focus and a hyperfocus on known products can limit innovation and the agility to adapt to changing market trends. Like a one-way mirror, companies that look only at their own reflection will fail to account for the world around them.**

- **How can companies respond to trends? What does it look like to walk the razor's edge of making timely adjustments without being blown about by the fickle and fleeting whims of consumers?**

If bottled ketchup and boxed macaroni and cheese bring back fond memories of favorite childhood meals, you're not alone. For years, packaged food giant Kraft Heinz skated by on these flagship products without a care in the world. And this approach worked — until it didn't.

In February 2019, Kraft Heinz reported a fourth-quarter net loss of $12.6 billion. After three years of stagnant sales, its stock tumbled by more than 20%. While many factors may have contributed to this significant decline, a noteworthy observation is the consumers' shift toward fresh food during this period. Some analysts suggest that Kraft Heinz could have been more aligned with this trend.

The company did make efforts to join the "fresh" movement, with initiatives like introducing the Oscar Mayer all-natural hot dog. However, these moves did not fully reverse the decline in sales.

To their detriment, some companies treat their market strategy like the one-way mirrors in police interrogation rooms: They only look at their own reflections, failing to account for the wider world around them.

A case of corporate myopia

Staying attuned to customers requires a broad vision. It demands an understanding of consumer desires and motivations that is enough to consider what their needs might be in the future. So why do some brands struggle to see beyond the here and now?

In the case of Kraft Heinz, a huge company with experience and informed leadership, the downward trend *actually* began back in 2014. While the rest of the world noticed consumer demands for healthier foods increasing, Kraft Heinz struggled with a case of corporate myopia.

One contributing factor to this issue may be too much internal focus that keep companies entrenched in their established practices. When a company is solely focused internally and on financial metrics and revenue, it can become more challenging to break away from what has always been done. This often results in a reluctance to innovate or replace traditional products with newer, more responsive alternatives that better align with evolving customer needs.

Hindsight is 20/20. It's simple to look back and see sweeping trends as obvious. But in the day-to-day operation of your business, the importance of trends isn't as plain to see, especially if you aren't actively looking for them. Business leaders also have a fine line to walk regarding trends. They need to assess which ones are illusionary blips and which constitute long-term, seismic market shifts.

The key is having a flexible, open mindset to consider multiple responses to trends — like the movement toward fresh foods, which happens to be one of those seismic shifts. From there, you need the processes, testing and agility to adapt accordingly.

How technology meets consumer needs in record time

Large corporations often prioritize efficiency and key metrics to such an extent that it stifles innovative and out-of-the-box thinking. While technology has brought about advancements across various industries, it has also accelerated the emergence of new market trends. This rapid change challenges brands to adapt swiftly, a task that can be at odds with a more traditional, metrics-driven approach.

Consumers' desire for convenience is nothing new. But streaming movies and taxi service at the tap of a button seemed like science fiction just 20 years ago. Today, technology provides the sudden leap forward to realize even the most far-fetched ambitions.

Prior to the digital revolution, barriers to entry were high enough to (somewhat) prevent new players from disrupting the status quo. Now, technology makes it easier than ever to break into a business or an industry, so new competitors can come from anywhere at any time.

This new reality demands a new skill set. Large corporations must learn to cannibalize themselves. Responding to market trends by finding new ways to replace your own business, even if it means launching new products, is the best way to adapt to consumer demands and stay relevant.

Unfortunately, in the case of Kraft Heinz, attempts to align with the fresh food movement, such as introducing 'all-natural hot dogs,' were viewed by some as merely superficial changes. Such efforts fell short of the radical self-reinvention that might have kept pace with evolving consumer preferences.

Keeping up with the (indirect) competition

Large packaged goods companies like Kraft Heinz should constantly — weekly or even *daily* — look at other packaged goods brands. This includes not just direct competitors but also indirect competitors that satisfy the same benefits for customers in completely different ways. These are the brands corporations should be most worried about.

To fully understand indirect competition just look at your cell phone. Smartphones have pretty much killed the alarm clock market, the consumer camera market, the portable music market and so on. The indirect competition offers the same benefit but in a different way. A few years ago if you wanted to enjoy the latest Hollywood film at home you took a trip to Blockbuster; now you stream it. Same outcome for you delivered in a more efficient way. The demise of Blockbuster highlights another reason why indirect competitors need to be monitored — direct competition can hurt you but indirect competition can kill you.

Food manufacturers like Kraft have operated a similar model for years. They create a range of foods to be purchased at the supermarket and prepared and consumed at home. Indirect competition to this model can be thought of as home delivery of takeout food such as Door Dash and Uber Eats. You could even see a move to reduce processed foods and cook more things from base ingredients as an indirect competitor. This would make Hello Fresh and the like potential indirect competitors.

Keeping at least one "rogue" company on your radar — an odd, indirect competitor that meets customer needs differently — is a key strategy for staying tuned into trends. This discipline allows businesses to pick up on changing consumer tastes and adapt when appropriate.

Whatever portion of their market research is focused on rogue competitors, companies need to keep this investigation ongoing. The key is a broad view, one that can account for trends without overcorrecting. A regular practice of scanning the horizon for trends and opportunities keeps you from chasing the latest thing and from remaining set in your ways. Choosing the latter option, as we've seen with Kraft Heinz, means consumers might leave you behind.

The venerable boxed-dinner and condiment behemoth isn't the only major brand left in the powdered cheese dust. Other corporations have also failed to respond to significant market changes, often due to internal disagreements among leadership over which trends to address in the first place.

By formalizing a decision-making process for adapting to trends, you can foster healthy testing and experimentation and maintain your volume of sales in the long run.

Scan the horizon and cannibalize yourself

What does it look like in practice when the teams behind successful brands keep their eyes on the horizon? They conduct research and gather information about trends.

When you've gathered enough data, be sure to incorporate plenty of collaboration into your meetings. Allow plenty of time for debate, discussion, analysis and agreement about how to proceed.

Experiment with new products that capture your customers' attention and meet their needs in new ways. Otherwise, your customers will pick someone else's product off the shelves.

And instead of macaroni and cheese or all-natural hot dogs, your competitors will eat *you* for lunch.

Click here or scan the QR code below to go to an episode of The Accidental Marketer where we discussed this one-way mirror, what went wrong for Kraft Heinz and how other brands can learn from their mistakes.

Link to Accidental Marketer Podcast

 **A Tool to Help Strategists Manage the Future: Trend Analysis**

Trend analysis is a straightforward two-step process. First, you identify relevant trends that may impact your business. Second, you prioritize the most important trends for further analysis and action. The idea is to prepare your business for potential futures rather than predict exactly what will happen. Conducting a robust trend analysis helps reduce vulnerability to unexpected surprises and enables quick responses when needed.

1. **Invite** a broad-based team to bring as many perspectives as possible to the table. Your goal is to generate a comprehensive list of potential future trends that will be prioritised later. Initially, you want to make sure to cover as many future scenarios as possible so invite people from outside your 'bubble'.

2. **Set** the scene so that all participants understand what is required. You are considering all possible future scenarios that could impact your business not trying to predict the future and narrowing it down too soon. The prioritize step will do that but for now, encourage people to think creatively.

3. **Start** by identifying as many future trends as possible. These could be trends that are already happening and forecasted to grow, such as the shift towards remote working and virtual meetings due to the pandemic, or trends that are just starting but expected to become significant in a short time, such as the use of AI for research or content writing. These trends could be industry-specific or more general, and it's important to identify as many as possible in this initial step. Two useful frameworks can help you generate potential trends.

a. The PEST framework stands for political, economic, social, and technological factors. Using this framework, consider trends in politics, economics, social/culture, and technology and how they might impact your business in the next few years.

b. Porter's five forces framework to assess industry profitability. The five forces are — the threat of new entrants, the threat of substitutes, the bargaining power of suppliers, the bargaining power of buyers, and existing competitive rivalry — which collectively shape the attractiveness of a market. While brainstorming, ask yourself and your team questions like, what new entrants could enter our market with a similar offer? What substitutes could enter our market addressing the same need but with a different offer? How might supplier power increase, leading to higher prices? How might buyer power increase, leading to lower prices? How will the existing competitive intensity change?

Regardless of the frameworks you use, the goal is to generate a long list of potential changes that could impact your market and business performance. Next, it's time to prioritize. For each identified trend, ask two questions: what would be the impact if this trend were to happen, and what is the likelihood of this trend happening?

4. **Consider** the impact and probability of occurrence of each trend on a scale of 1 to 10.

a. Assess the probability of each trend happening on a scale of 1 to 10, where 1 signifies extremely unlikely and 10 signifies almost certain.

> b. Assess the potential impact on your business should the forecast trend become reality. Again use a ten-point scale where 1 signifies very little impact and 10 signifies a major impact.
>
> c. Once you have scored each trend for impact and probability, plot the results on a chart. Use the vertical axis to represent the magnitude of impact (from 1 to 10) and the horizontal axis to represent the probability or likelihood (from 1 to 10). Plot each trend on the chart, using numbers to represent the trends for clarity.
>
> 5. **Focus** on the trends that appear in the top right of the chart, which have high impact and high probability. These are the most important trends to consider in your strategic planning. However, do not ignore trends with high impact and low probability or low impact and high probability — these should also be considered, even if you ultimately decide not to act.

Click here or use the QR code below to download an electronic version of the Trends tool

Link to Trends tool

Chapter 2.
How Do You Stay Attuned to Power Shifts In Your Industry?

Featured Case: Pharmaceutical Brand, GE & Air Conditioners

Tool: Influencer Map

Key Takeaways:

- **When working with brands — especially in mature markets, marketers may be tempted to assume they know their stakeholders and the level of influence those stakeholders wield. But this is a mistake: Markets are *always* changing, and those who don't tune in will be left behind.**

- **By creating an influencer map and regularly revisiting any influence shifts in your industry, you position yourself to assess and adjust what you need to change to maintain your market share.**

- **Why is influencer mapping so important? Who should be a part of this key conversation? And how do you make time for *another* process in your busy schedule?**

When setting out on any journey, you first need the lay of the land. If you're heading on an old-school road trip (without the aid of Waze or Google Maps), you need a map. If you're a brand looking to gain and/or maintain market share, you need an Influencer Map. But if you've ever used an inaccurate or outdated map, you *probably* didn't arrive at your destination as planned. In the same way, when your audience intel doesn't keep up with ongoing power shifts, you're bound to lose market share *fast*, especially in mature markets — where loss of exclusivity or loss of differentiation is imminent.

The Case of the Pharmaceutical Brand

This pitfall poses a danger to pharmaceutical enterprises and non-pharma brands alike. The team behind one pharmaceutical hypertension brand was concerned because they were rapidly losing market share. They analyzed their ability to compete — and realized they *should* have been winning in the market because doctors preferred their brand and claimed that they prescribed their medication most often. Instead, the reality was that the company was rapidly losing market share. So, the team began to explore the disconnect by analyzing an Influencer Map, which revealed some unexpected insights.

While doctors were favorable to the drug, their overall influence on the buying decision was shrinking. Instead, considerable power was shifting to pharmacies and patients/care givers. Neither of these stakeholder groups saw the unique value of the hypertension drug (or the company). Armed with this understanding, the company's marketers further explored the needs of the pharmacies, especially the pharmacy managers, and found ways to partner with them to better inform and support patients/care givers. This also required shifting some of their resources and redeploying their sales force. The new plan did, in fact, reverse the falling market shares.

Often it is clear who the ultimate decision maker is in a buying situation — such as the doctors in this case. So, you don't want to ignore them. However, when you identify the influencers (or the people who can impact the decision makers), and you allocate a portion of your efforts and resources to them, this should open up more opportunities for your company.

The Case of GE's Headquarters

When General Electric (GE) was looking to establish its European headquarters, it settled in London. It seemed to be a logical choice given that people spoke English and that it was considered a leading international business and travel hub. When GE tried to purchase Honeywell, the US regulators approved the purchase, however, the EU regulators rejected the deal. What happened? Probably many things. Even a simple Influencer Map would have shown that the EU Regulators were one of the biggest decision makers for GE's acquisitions and business deals — and they weren't located in London, which put GE at a disadvantage. Once GE sorted this out, they not only moved to Brussels where the EU Regulators are located, but they established themselves in the same business complex. So, when GE employees went for coffee and lunch — they were able to start establishing relationships. Moving forward, most of GE's European acquisitions were successful.

This illustrates that an Influencer Map can be valuable at any level in the organization — including the highest level where companies are making significant investment decisions.

A manufacturer of commercial air-conditioning units was unable to create a differential advantage by strengthening its distribution and service functions — at best it was playing catch up to the market leader. So, they decided to develop a line of sturdy, quiet, highly reliable but expensive home air conditioning units. The product was well made (design engineering being a critical capability they possessed) and tested well with prospective customers, even at the premium price point. But they failed to sell in sufficient numbers. The reason was the weight of the unit. The distribution and installation companies, who had a huge influence over the customer's choice, could not install them with a typical one or two-person crew. This meant they pretty much refused to stock the new unit. By missing the critical influence of distribution and installation companies, they created a great product that would never be sold.

One of the themes that you hopefully see from these cases it's a mistake to underestimate or miss anyone in your influence analysis. The pharmaceutical company had not made the pharmacy managers a priority, GE was missing the impact of the EU Regulators, and the air conditioning company missed the influence of the installation crew. But the power of these "hidden influencers" can't be overstated, and it's incumbent upon brands to create influencer maps that show who holds the power — not just one time, but continually.

Turn and face the strange ch-ch-changes

As cliche as it may be, the only constant truly is change. Market changes happen for a variety of reasons, such as a new trend that emerges or a competitor reaching a key audience with a new value proposition, message or incentive. Before you know it, the ground beneath your feet shifts unexpectedly. An Influencer Map, when updated frequently, can serve as an early warning system when changes are on the way.

The value of influencer mapping is that it can help capture how markets — even mature ones — evolve over time. For example, in maturing markets we often see power shift from the medical or technical experts to purchasing/buying groups within customer companies. The sales team calling on these customers, therefore are required to gain new skills and shift their focus and messages.

You and your team might think you know your business and its stakeholders backward and forward. However, it's a trap to let your expertise distract you from the discipline of regularly examining power shifts among market influencers.

Who should be invited?

When asked who should be invited to an Influencer mapping work session, we have a saying: "anyone who can mess up your plans later — should be included early". The more voices that contribute, the more likely you are to detect the power shifts that will help you keep market share and possibly provide unique opportunities. Often, we find that colleagues are more supportive of plans because they were initially involved. Ironically, there's an *internal Influencer Map* that is always working in the background that's important to consider.

So, when deciding who to bring into the conversation, consider other functions that touch the market space. For example, bringing salespeople into the fold can spark valuable insights from their direct, daily interactions with customers. For the same reason, customer support teams provide an understanding of the questions and pain points your audience experiences. Medical & technical people often attend conferences and talk with their peers from other companies so they have an unique view of potential trends and competitor movements. Legal and finance are trained to identify the risks — which is helpful to fully vetting the current and future market. The combination of these unique perspectives can shed light on multiple stages of the customer lifecycle and help detect subtle but important changes on the horizon.

[Click here](#) or use the QR code below to go to an episode of the Accidental Marketer, where we discuss best practices for every brand to understand industry stakeholders amidst an ever-changing market.

Link to Accidental Marketer Podcast

 **A Tool to Help Market Leaders Think Differently: The Influencer Map (aka Stakeholder Map).**

How to create your Influencer Map

1. **Invite** a cross-functional group of colleagues so that you have a broad perspective of the market. For example, medical & technical people, finance, sales, customer support and service. Plan for about 2 hours. (Note: food and drinks always provide greater incentives for people to attend).

2. **Scope** the project in terms of what decisions are you trying to make (e.g., how do we enter the European market and become a viable player within 5 years)? Make sure that everyone is aligned with the scope.

3. **Brainstorm** all the possible decision makers and influencers that currently exist in the market. These may be buyers and non-buyers. Don't miss anyone.

   a. Remember that this is an *external* view of the market — so you don't include your <u>internal</u> stakeholders (you can create a separate internal Influencer Map if necessary). Do not include your sales people — they are resources that you will decide to deploy based on results.

   b. The list should be of <u>people</u> (a person whose "door" you could potentially knock on). If you find that there are some important trends — get underneath it and identify the <u>people</u> that may be generating or impacting the trend.

   c. Don't include <u>competitors</u> — while they can also influence the market, they (like you) are taking an outside perspective on where to focus their efforts. (An advanced version of this is to war game how competitors see the market).

4. Draw your Influencer Map

   a. Magnitude of Influence — from your list, draw circles for each stakeholder identified based on which influencers <u>currently</u> have:

      i. Significant power over the decision — they will have the largest circles.

      ii. Moderate power over the decision — they will have medium sized circles.

      iii. Very low or no power over the decision — they will have very small sized circles.

   b. Shifts in Power — now considering the <u>future</u> (e.g., 2-5 years; the timeframe determined in your scope).

      i. Influence is *growing* — draw a dotted line outside the circle.

      ii. Influence is *shrinking* — draw a dotted line inside the circle

      iii. Influence is *neutral* — no need to draw additional lines.

c. Additional notes on your map:

    i. You can group people together into a mega circle if it makes sense (e.g., different functions that work in the hospital) — but still indicate their level of influence within the mega circle.

    ii. The shifts in power should balance — it's a net-zero. Meaning that even in the future, there is still one buying decision. Example, you may have a large influencer that is shrinking, and two smaller influencers that are growing. There shouldn't be a case where everyone is growing or everyone is shrinking.

d. **Communications between influencers** — add arrows to indicate how each stakeholder influences other stakeholders. Sometimes the influence is light (dotted arrows). The influence often works bidirectionally, with each stakeholder influencing the other — this is indicated by double-tipped arrows. Sometimes the influence goes in only one direction (single-tipped arrow).

5. **Analysis and Prioritization** — Once the map is drawn, the real work begins; determining resource decisions based on the map. You do this by asking two questions: Who were the top three stakeholders/influencers, in terms of allocating marketing and sales time and effort *prior to this analysis*? Then, how should our priorities change, *based on the Influence Map*?

[Click here](#) or use the QR code below to download an electronic version of the Influencer Map tool

Link to the Influencer Map tool

Continuous Thinking Tool

Because of the value of an Influencer Map to warn of upcoming changes, it's important to treat it as a *proactive* tool rather than a *reactive* one.

It doesn't change *completely* from year to year. However, if you're not changing *anything* from year to year, you might not be looking deeply enough to understand the hidden influencers affecting the market.

If you keep your versions of your Influencer Map over time — you can see how correct (or incorrect) you and your team were — this may help you better predict the future.

It is important to not only gain insights regarding the shifts in influence, but to reallocate resources accordingly. This could look like shifting focus toward some stakeholders and away from others. Using Influencer Maps is an organizational skill that can improve your company's ability to maintain or grow market share over time.

Chapter 3.
How Do Innovators Keep Their Edge?

Featured Case: Haier and The Cold Case of the Cool Takeover

Tool: Benefits Ladder and Vietnam Card Sort

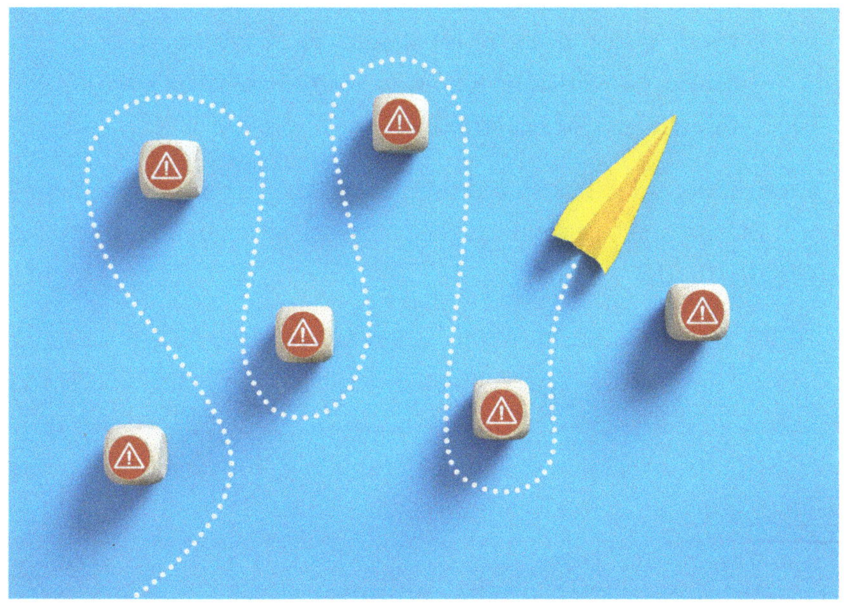

Key Takeaways:

- **Haier Appliances just might be one of the most customer focused B2B brands in the world. The Qingdao, China-based manufacturer, which claims the largest worldwide market share among appliance brands, acquired GE's appliance business in 2016.**

- **Through multiple eras of innovation and reinvention, Haier has had a single CEO at its helm for nearly three decades. Over the years, the company solidified its place in the market by becoming zealously customer-centric and by effectively developing new products in response to consumer needs.**

- **How can stalwart industries continue to innovate? What does it look like to reinvent your brand continually *and* stay rooted in your core offerings (and leadership)?**

You know your household appliances keep you and your food cold. But do you know which company has been making them *cool* since the 1980s?

GE's appliance business was acquired by a brand whose name you may have never heard. Qingdao, China-based Haier Appliances (pronounced like "higher") has been sweeping — rather, *blowing* — through the appliance space with innovative air conditioners and college dorm refrigerators for decades.

Today, Haier holds the largest worldwide market share of the home appliances industry. While that's impressive enough, what happens behind the scenes may be even more remarkable. Its CEO, Zhang Ruimin, has been in his position for nearly 30 years. (He's clearly doing something right.)

Haier just might be the most customer centric B2B organization in the world. With a thriving B2C line of business as well, the company demands the fear and respect of its industry competitors — and delights its many customers who use its appliances daily.

Haier is living proof that a long-standing and even stodgy industry is always ready for the innovation and reinvention of a focused, fearless brand.

Eras of reinvention

Haier has been busy carving out its customer-centric niche in the appliance industry for decades. That kind of distinction doesn't come without transition, innovation, and evolutions that respond to changing markets and customer needs.

Over the years, the company spotted opportunities to create products for niche audiences, like the wine refrigerators it developed in the early 2000s. When Haier noted that wine connoisseurs valued wine temperature control, it responded accordingly and so did its customers.

Haier pivoted in four distinct areas for four eras of reinvention.

In the 1980s, quality was a major weakness for a majority of appliance manufacturers. Haier differentiated itself by focusing on product quality *and* made waves by changing consumers' perception of what makes a quality appliance.

Haier made the ultimate power move toward becoming customer-centric brand in the 1990s, creating specialized teams to focus on the needs of specific customers. When a customer (who happened to be a farmer) called to complain about too much dirt in their washing machine, Haier's customer team didn't write off the concern. Instead, they worked to understand the customer's need.

As it turned out, this customer used his washer in an unconventional way: farmers make more money when their produce is clean. Haier *then* developed a new product in response to the problem: a machine for washing vegetables.

The company's next evolution came in the 2000s when it looked inward, learning to build self-managing teams and improve decision-making. While many companies struggle with balancing organizational needs and consumer needs, Haier made the integration of both its top priority. The needs of its audience went hand-in-hand with operating norms that maintained the company's customer focus.

The fourth era (and most recent pivot) for Haier was learning to become a truly digital company. Plenty of brands procrastinate making this transition, yet Haier not only adjusted to the change but embraced it. Today, the company thrives in an increasingly digital marketplace.

Looking to "Haier" leadership

While Haier's decision to keep reinventing itself is remarkable, what's *more* extraordinary is the fact that it has had one CEO throughout those significant changes. There are wins *and* drawbacks that come with such a long tenure of senior leadership, but Haier's success is certainly a feather in Ruimin's cap.

So, what does it take for an organization to retain just one successful CEO for decades? First things first: consistency. Just as a veteran sports coach needs a winning record, a long-term CEO needs a track record leading the business toward success and steady achievement.

Consistency can spark a virtuous cycle: Success spawns a team that is more confident in the CEO's decisions and leadership — which, in turn, leads to further success.

What's more, when the same leader stays at the helm for a significant amount of time, they develop a stronger sense of their vision for the organization. From there, the CEO can hire and promote more personnel that fit that vision. Through the years, Ruimin has stayed zealous, both for customer service and for keeping his team engaged and innovative.

Many organizations are quick to ignore the necessary learning curve for a leader, and they make a change when a CEO doesn't deliver results right away. Moreover, no business can *always* be on top; waning success, at times, is inevitable. But being too quick to remove a CEO fails to consider the longer term. Haier has kept its attention on the big picture — in both keeping Ruimin as CEO and creating its market strategy — and has been rewarded.

Two forms of innovation

In recent years, Haier surveyed thousands of customers about their thoughts on air conditioning. One of its major findings was that people want A/C to cool them down but not make them *cold*.

After reviewing online conversations, Haier directly implemented consumer feedback when designing new products. The company's engineers refined air conditioners' function to make air "cool, not cold" (which became its brand positioning). They also added light indicators for air quality and visually redesigned the units.

This is a perfect example of one of the two forms of innovation that Haier has mastered: listening to customers and implementing their feedback.

The second form of innovation that Haier perfected is "future-building." Improvements in A/C units' air quality and cleaning functions didn't come from direct feedback via customer surveys. Rather, the Haier team looked at larger-scale trends in China to understand that consumers' concerns about air quality were growing.

From there, they made projections based on that trend and built the air quality feature into Haier products as something its *future* customer would want. The feature became hugely popular, and this "future-building" innovation paid off.

Always climbing *higher*

Haier is the ideal reminder that even a business in an industry that seems set in its ways can chart a new course by listening and responding to customers. Modern, forward-thinking practices can tap into massive market opportunities that are otherwise untouched.

In addition to looking outward at consumer audiences, look inward and trust the process. Just as the CEO trusts their team to work well within their specialties, organizations should trust the CEO to lead through multiple eras and successfully reinvent the company over time.

Even when the competition heats up, you'll be able to keep your cool — *and* your share of the market.

Click here or use the QR code below to go to the episode of the Accidental Marketer podcast where we dove into what Haier has been doing right for decades, and you just might glean a few insights to "apply" to your organization, too.

Link to Accidental Marketer Podcast

All of Haier's innovation successes in their markets were rooted in an essential discipline: understanding customer needs. At some companies, discussions about customer needs are overshadowed by inwardly focused dialogue concerning product features; others overlook customers to obsess over competitor's moves. But a close look at companies like Haier will reveal a relentless practice of not only uncovering today's customer requirements, but anticipating how these will change in the future (see Haier's "future-building" initiative above.)

How does an organization form a common language and approach in mastering the art of uncovering current and future customer needs? We have seen no better tool than the deceptively simple Benefits Ladder. By understanding the definitions of each "rung" in the ladder — and by consistently updating the tool through continuous dialogue with customers — companies will understand their market share success (or lack of it), gain valuable insights into how to better communicate with customers, and anticipate the future customer desires that fuel successful innovation.

 **Tools to Help Innovators Keep Their Edge: Benefits Ladder and the Vietnam Card Sort**

How To Build a Benefits Ladder

To build a Benefits Ladder (click the link or QR code to see what a Benefits Ladder looks like), one must understand each level or "rung" in it. Attributes are product or service features that customers want or desire. Benefits are the rational, measurable outcomes customers are seeking. Values are sometimes irrational, always emotional motives that customers have.

Ironically, starting at the bottom of the ladder is a trap because customers rarely care about or talk in terms of attributes. Here is how we suggest you proceed:

1. **Start** at the middle level, highlighting the most important benefits that customers seek. Benefits are rational, measurable outcomes that customers are seeking, and customers typically talk in the language of benefits. Imagine customers saying "I like to work with companies that help me to…." The completion of that statement will yield many important benefits. We call this the "help me to…" technique.

2. Then, move up a rung and list all of the values you can think of by asking "why is this benefit important?" until you land on an emotion. Values are not the language that customers typically talk in, but they point towards deep-rooted motivators that drive buying behavior.

3. Finally, list the attributes of your product or service that support the benefits and values you've highlighted; and list and circle new attributes that you could develop to fulfill important customer benefits and values.

Click here or use the QR code below to download an electronic version of the Benefits Ladder tool.

Link to Benefits Ladder tool

The Vietnam Card Sort: The logical question, of course, is "how do you get a Benefits Ladder right?" Many marketers and sales reps have had the experience of asking customers "what are your needs?" only to be met with a blank stare, or obvious answers like "lower price" or "faster delivery."

Many of our clients have overcome this issue by using a technique we call the Vietnam Card Sort. The "Vietnam" part comes from the fact that we first successfully tested this technique in that beautiful country for an agricultural products company, and the card sort part will become obvious in the following explanation.

How to Use a Vietnam Card Sort (or click on the link to the video below)

1.   **Create** a hypothesis of 5-6 customer benefits using the "help me to…" technique.

2. **List** each of these benefits on an individual index card and add a couple of blank cards to your stack.

3. **Explain** to the customer that you are trying to understand them better and that you've created a hypothesis that is "probably wrong."

4. **Put** the index cards in front of them and ask them to tell you which ones resonate, which ones are wrong, and which needs you have missed.

5. **Write** down any needs you've missed on the blank index cards you've brought along.

6. **If** you have time, ask them to put the cards which reflect their real needs in the order of importance to them.

Step 6 will help you with the segmentation tool in the next chapter

[Click here](#) or use the QR Code Below to View the Vietnam Card Sort Video

Link to Vietnam Card Sort video

You will be surprised at how few Vietnam Card Sorts you have to do before recognizing some consistent patterns in customer needs. You will also be amazed at the richness of the conversations, especially if your past customer needs inquiries have been very general. And through recognizing the patterns, you will gain tremendous confidence that you are "getting it right" when it comes to customer needs — a pre-requisite to any marketing success.

With the combination of the Benefits Ladder and Vietnam Card sort tools, you and your organization can become world-class at the crucial skill of understanding customer needs.

Chapter 4.
How Do Traditional Businesses Keep Up With New Digital Competitors?

Featured Case: Uber, Airbnb and The Case of the Digital Chokepoint

Tool: Needs-Based Segmentation

Key Takeaways:

- **The digital age has brought major changes to virtually every industry. Technology has lowered the barrier to entry for large swaths of new competitors who monetize the channels between consumers and goods in a "digital chokepoint."**

- **While digital transformation has drastically changed the way we do business and meet customer needs, traditional businesses have an advantage with customers who prioritize quality or intimacy.**

- **How can traditional brands stand their ground in the face of new upstart competitors? The not-so-secret weapon is listening to your customers and solving any friction in their experiences.**

What do Uber, Airbnb and Amazon have in common? For one thing, they've each taken long-established industries — on-demand transportation, hospitality and retail — by storm. And they've done so not through traditional pathways (which typically require specialized assets and skills), but through digital means.

The Digital Age has ushered in rapid changes in all spheres of life and business. Technological advancements now make it possible to digitally control *and* monetize the access point between consumers and their desired goods — leading to what we're calling the "digital chokepoint."

For virtually every industry, this sea change doesn't just mean a massive increase in competition as third parties move in. It also means these new competitors are performing higher-margin services — without owning taxi cabs, hotels or retail space.

The digital chokepoint forces traditional competitors to take a long, hard look at how they'll keep up with the changing times.

'Right of way': Not a novel concept

The digital chokepoint is, ultimately, a change in "right of way" — owning a channel between Point A to Point B. And it's far from the first time in history that we've seen such a monumental shift.

For instance, Railroad companies in the USA owned significant rights of way between cities and states. Building railroads across the United States was a massive effort that couldn't have happened without government cooperation. The work required changes in immigration law to support labor, military support to protect assets and the use of eminent domain to claim the land for the rails.

Because the railway companies owned the right of way, they had substantial power, and telegraph companies took advantage. The two industries made a trade: free telegraph usage for railroad companies in exchange for access to install telegraph poles along train lines. But this deal underestimated right-of-way power. If monetized fully, railways could have owned the telecommunications industry outright as well.

Now, with digital "right of way" up for grabs — including access to control of information and the customer journey — innovative technologies offer new competitors billions of dollars of opportunities across the global marketplace.

Before the impact of digital platforms, major taxi services had their industry locked up. But the Ubers and Lyfts of the world were able to change the game, not just via their digital platforms but also through legal means. By changing restrictions, they significantly lowered the barriers to entry that traditional taxi companies historically faced and exploded right of way for the vehicle-for-hire industry.

The digital chokepoint raises complex questions about ownership. For instance, do companies or customers truly *own* the data they collect? Whatever the answer, for those up to the challenge of making complex industries simple through digital control of access points, the business potential is unlimited.

The strengths of traditional competitors

With such drastic digital adjustments taking place, many traditional businesses may find it difficult to determine how to adapt. Should they switch their approach to match their new competitors? Or should they lean into the rights of way they already have?

First things first: Remember that even where digital means intercept supply and demand, there is no replacement for customer intimacy. Directly delivering a service to the customer brings an incomparable depth of understanding about customer needs. For customers, value comes from your solution not just meeting their demands but *how* you meet them.

Lock onto the strength of your service and personalization — and look for key differentiators you offer in the areas where you can't compete with digital solutions. Consider the major points of friction in your industry for your customers. Reduce your vulnerability to new competitors by finding ways to better the customer experience by removing those points of friction. Then, implement those improvements before your competitors have a chance.

Here's the good news: Some segments of your customer base are drawn to the intimacy they have with you because they've been using your service for quite some time. You know a lot about these customers, and you can use that information to improve their experience in a way your competitors can't. Distinguish yourself as *the* choice for these intimacy-seeking customers.

Another segment in which to fine-tune your approach: the quality-focused segments of your audience. Which of your customers places a high value on working with companies that control the assets of production? They won't be easily swayed by the Amazons and Alibabas of the world because they're focused on quality — and they know they'll get the highest possible quality from you.

Responding to the digital chokepoint

The massive shifts brought on by the digital marketplace continue apace as new competitors change their approaches. So B2B companies must take strategic steps to adapt in ways that match their evolving industries.

First, gather insights about your customers and their experiences. To resolve their friction points, you need to uncover them. Conducting a "day in the life" assessment as a great way to do just that.

Ask someone from another part of your business (who doesn't have the same biases or background as you) to watch your customers for a day or more. A fresh set of eyes can do a world of good to help you understand their wins and their pain points. You might see problems you take for granted, especially if you've been in your line of business for a long time.

Another way to uncover friction points is through complaint discovery — a technique of engaging with past/current customers to ask what frustrates them about doing business with you. The conversation cannot end until the customer mentions at least 3 complaints, and includes a discussion of what could be done to eliminate the causes of this friction.

What kinds of frustrations do your customers express that reveal solvable friction points? To keep up with your new "upstart" competitors, listen to your customers. It's the best long-term strategy to find ways to improve their experience in ways that no one else can.

While the quality-seeking and intimacy-driven segments of your customers are a great short-term focus, you shouldn't see their business as a perennial solution to an ever-changing industry.

The way forward: safeguarding your business

Technology means more threat than thrill for many traditional companies that met their customers' needs for years. As the saying goes, they've forgotten more than newer "uberized" companies will ever know about the business.

If you've been talking about these types of customer-focused adjustments for years, now is the time to actually implement them. Making changes that better serve your customers and solve their problems is the best course to protect your business — and make you less vulnerable to disaggregation by third-party competition.

That way, you'll be able to hold out instead of being choked out.

Click here or use the QR code below to go to an the episode of the Accidental Marketer, where we discuss the impacts of these changes for B2B companies, how traditional competitors can lean into their strengths and what to do to avoid getting "choked out" yourself.

Link to Accidental Marketer Podcast

 **Tools to Keep Up with New Digital Competitors: Needs-Based Segmentation and Targeting**

In the previous chapter, we wrote about how Haier's strategy was propelled by their deep understanding of changing customer needs. Techniques like the Vietnam Card Sort, and tools like the Benefits Ladder — both covered in Chapter 3 — are highly-applicable and necessary if you are facing (or creating) digital chokepoints in your industry. In fact, due to the greater number of stakeholders when selling to another business (a B2B scenario instead of Haier's B2C case), building several Benefits Ladders — one for each key stakeholder — is advisable.

You need a specific application of these techniques and tools in the industry-disrupting circumstances like those highlighted in this chapter. Innovators like Airbnb, Uber and Amazon have gained control of access points between buyers and the goods and services they seek in their industries, and someone may be attempting or accomplishing the same thing in yours.

So, your benefits-uncovering activities for these situations must focus on finding friction and frustration in the current buyer experience. As we suggest above, use techniques like "Day in the Life" and "complaint discovery" to uncover buyer issues, just like Uber or Airbnb would. This emphasis will create a Benefits Ladder that highlights a range of needs; as well as opportunities to remove friction and (re)take control of the digital chokepoint in your industry. This is why you should read the previous chapter on Haier and the related tools section, then come back here to learn how you can build on these concepts in using the tools.

Why Segment?: Need-Based Segmentation is the process of dividing customer into groups — based on their needs. All the members of a segment have similar needs, but these needs are different from those of other segments.

By understanding the needs that drive each segment, we can target those that will likely appreciate our value propositions more — and even improve our value propositions based on our findings. And we can also spend less time with those segments not likely to choose our offer over competitors.

Segmentation makes our sales and marketing activities more efficient and effective. It can also lead us to create new products or services based on diving deeper into a segment's needs.

Ultimately, segmentation uncovers opportunities hidden in broad-brush approaches to markets.

How To Segment and Target (NOTE: you might find it necessary to view the downloadable version of the Segmentation tool in order to properly follow the instructions below):

1. **Use** the top 5 benefits sought from the Benefits Ladder activity summarized in the previous chapter.

2. **Configure** 5 different segments by hypothesizing how different types of customers would rank the importance of each benefit differently. Assume, that there might a segment that would rank each of the five benefits as "most important" — we call this the "diagonal ones" method.

3. **These** different configurations of benefits sought rankings quickly identify 4-5 possible different segments. Talk to your salesforce or custome contact personnel to determine if all 5 segments exist — eliminate those that do not exist (hint: most and maybe all of them will be valid!)

4. **It's** likely that after analyzing these 4-5 different segments, one segment would be the equivalent of the "quality-seeking" group identified above, and another would represent the previously mentioned "intimacy-driven" cohort.

5. **The** other 2-3 segments would be driven by needs that are based on your discovery of friction points in the buyer experience (See "Additional Targeting Comments").

6. **Knowing** which segments to target would be a function of your company's capabilities.

[Click here](#) or use the QR code below to download an electronic version of the Segmentation tool

Link to the Segmentation tool

Additional Targeting Comments: If you are a traditional competitor with limited abilities to take control of the digital chokepoint, you would likely compete fiercely for the quality and intimacy segments. They will likely be where you have an advantage.

If you are an industry disrupter, you would focus on segments defined by the main frustrations with the current customer experience. And if you are somewhere in the middle of these two, you might pursue one or a couple of segments from either group. It all comes down to how well your capabilities match with what each segment wants.

Chapter 5.
How Do Market Leaders Think Differently About Competition?

Featured Case: Amazon/Kohl's and The Case of the Symbiotic Competitor

Tool: Competitor Identification

Key Takeaways:

- All Kohl's stores started accepting and packaging Amazon returns, at no cost to the customer, and shipping them to Amazon fulfilment centers.

- This partnership has clear benefits for Kohl's — mainly a supply of dissatisfied Amazon customers streaming into their stores — but it's less obvious what notoriously competitive Amazon is getting from it.

- Is forming a partnership the new acquisition? Instead of buying a smaller company with a particular set of skills, could larger companies get more out of teaming up with them?

The point of having competitors is typically to defeat them. That's the way it is with sports, politics and pie-eating contests, and that's the way it typically is with business. So why has the most ruthless of business competitors apparently teamed up with a rival?

In 2017, department chain Kohl's announced that 82 of its stores in LA and Chicago would start accepting Amazon returns. Customers wouldn't even have to go to the trouble of forcing their no-good product back into its box. Kohl's would repackage the products destined for return, and ship them back to Amazon, all at no charge to the customer. It must have worked: in 2019, Kohl's extended the service to all of its 1,150+ stores nationwide. (Except Anchorage, Alaska. Sorry, northern friends.)

This partnership has raised eyebrows. Amazon and the ecommerce movement it helped create was the David that took down the department store Goliaths. As recently as 2016, without mentioning Amazon directly, Kohl's announced that it would be closing 18 stores, ultimately replacing them with smaller ones.

It seems that there's no bitterness on Kohl's end. But what is each of these competitors getting from their partnership?

Kohl's looks like a winner in this arrangement

The lion share of the benefits of this deal seem to be going to Kohl's.

At the top level, Amazon is effectively sending customers into Kohl's stores. And not just any customers: customers who were so unimpressed with the merchandise they bought from Amazon that they're willing to go through the process of returning it.

To frame it from the other side, Kohl's is laying out the welcome mat for the people Amazon failed to serve effectively, at the exact moment when their frustration with Amazon is at its peak.

Not only that, but the grumpy person holding their broken Amazon toaster probably still needs a toaster. If they can find a replacement in Kohl's, they're primed to buy it. To capitalize on this irritation even further, Kohl's has historically offered coupons to customers doing Amazon returns at their stores.

Kohl's does have to cover the cost of repacking and shipping the returned packages to Amazon. But the numbers seem to be playing out how the company anticipated. Two years into the trial, participating Chicago Kohl's stores brought in more sales than the department chain's nationwide average, and saw a 9% increase in new customers between 2017 and 2018, compared to a nationwide average increase of 1%.

Untangling what Amazons gets out of this partnership

Kohl's incentive for the partnership is clear — customer acquisition. But the benefits to Amazon are a little muddier.

To say that Amazon is not known for having a friendly attitude towards competitors is like saying that Jeff Bezos is quite rich. Stories about Amazon's relationship with competing brands typically make free use of words like "crushing," "steamrolling," "ruthless" and "brutally competitive."

So why is Amazon participating in a scheme that, at least on the surface, clearly benefits a competitor?

One possibility is that this is a well-disguised trick designed to gather information about Kohl's, so Amazon can take it down from the inside. A Trojan horse approach, if you will. Perhaps Amazon is using its Kohl's partnership to test customers' preferred return methods, before it invests in more of its own brick-and-mortar stores.

Another potential explanation is that Amazon understands that a certain segment of its customers are befuddled by the concept of returning a package to a website, and prefer an in-person return experience — especially one that takes care of the repackaging.

Amazon's reach is now so broad that its customer base extends beyond the tech-savvy. It's serving people who've never used Facebook, but are grateful for the convenience of ordering denture cream online. Many people in this demographic grew up thinking of the department store as the one place that has everything. The Kohl's/Amazon partnership associates the latter with the former, and in doing so, it highlights Amazon as the more convenient, 21st-century version of something people already understand.

Maybe Amazon really has accepted that Kohl's has staying power, and it's time to work with it, not against it. Equally likely, we just haven't seen its plan come to fruition yet.

The Kohl's/Amazon partnership isn't the only example of competitors teaming up

As surprising as this partnership is, there are other examples of competitors working together to offer customers a better experience, which ultimately benefits both rivals.

This is especially true in technology. For example, the home security space often sees multiple companies providing open source software that can work with their competitors' offerings, because customers want everything to be able to talk to each other.

There's also the more traditional version of the rival becoming the ally, in which the bigger company buys out the smaller one that does something the bigger company doesn't have the tech to do yet.

In some ways, the Kohl's/Amazon deal is a new iteration of the acquisition. Both companies are using each other to add a value proposition they can't offer on their own.

Kohl's cannot compete with Amazon's ability to attract online customers — so it picks up the ones who aren't happy with Amazon's service. And Amazon doesn't have enough brick-and-mortar stores to offer in-person returns: not yet, anyway.

By joining forces, both companies get to stay separate, while also adding benefits to entice customers.

Be open-minded about working with your competitors

The lesson from this interesting example of competitors throwing aside their differences and skipping hand-in-hand through a field of customer returns is that you should be open-minded about partnerships that can help you improve your customers' experiences. Even when it involves teaming up with a rival.

Bottom line: We don't entirely understand Amazon's motives for this deal. The company's track record suggests a partner like Kohl's should be cautious — even though the legacy department store has benefited from the partnership so far. And both companies have something to gain.

Maybe this is less a Trojan horse than a cash cow.

[Click here](#) or use the QR code below to go to an the episode of the Accidental Marketer, we discussed the pros and cons for Amazon and Kohl's, and whether this could mark a move towards a more symbiotic approach between competing companies.

Link to Accidental Marketer Podcast

A Tool to Help Market Leaders Think Differently: Competitor Identification

We've noticed that sometimes our clients get their biggest ideas and strategies from some of our simpler tools. Many "aha" moments have come from using the very straightforward Competitor Identification tool. These insights typically come from the less obvious, harder-to-complete parts of the tool, so dig into those pieces diligently!

How To Create Competitor Identification

The Competitor ID matrix includes six different inputs. There are three main categories to identify: Direct Competitors, Indirect Competitors, and Complementors.

1. **List Actual Direct Competitors** — companies that compete with you today, using the same type of process or form of offer.

2. **Identify Potential Direct Competitors** — companies that could become direct competitors if they wanted to enter your industry.

3. **Next write down all of the Indirect Actual Competitors you can think of** — companies that fulfill the same needs and functions as your offer does but use different processes or technologies.

4. **List Indirect Potential Competitors next.** Sometimes they are difficult to identify, but most of this category is made up of new types of technologies that could potentially revolutionize an industry.

5. **Identify Actual Complementors next** — they offer products that work with your solutions in a non-competitive way.

6. **Finally, write down Potential Complementors** — complementors that you are not currently working with.

[Click here](#) or use the QR code below to download an electronic version of the Competitor ID tool

Link to the Competitor ID tool

When it comes to "coopetition" opportunities like those high-lighted in the Amazon/Kohl's case, Direct Competitors are usually the least likely category for you to consider; but potential direct competitors and indirect actual competitors can be great candidates for partnerships or acquisitions. Actual complementors are already working with your company, while potential complementors are companies that you are not currently working with.

Be exhaustive in this process! It is important to identify all competitors to make sure your value proposition is better than those of rivals so you can maintain and grow market share. And be open-minded to opportunities to creatively form partnerships that benefit your customers and your company.

Chapter 6.
How Can Market Research Help Avoid Disaster and Drive Success?

Featured Case: Lexus/Phaeton and The Case of the Divergent Paths

Tools: Ability to Win

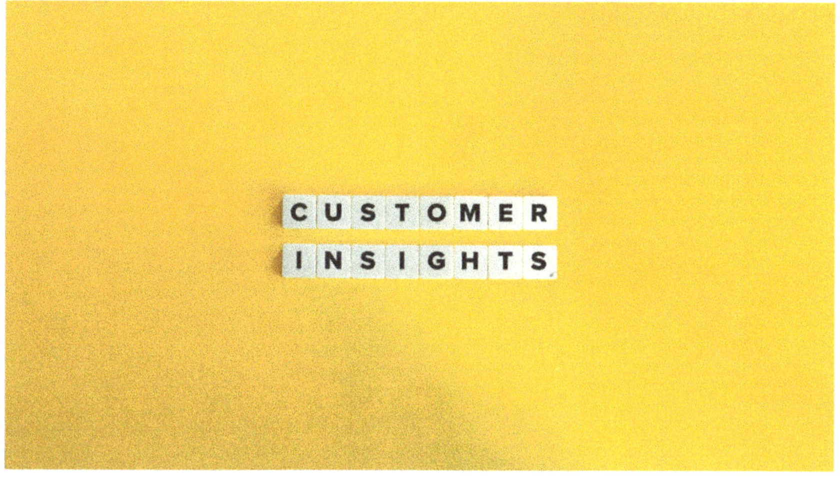

Key Takeaways:

- **Two auto brands set out on a journey to produce a luxury vehicle. Toyota's Lexus was a smashing success, while Volkswagen's Phaeton is seen as one of the major failures of the auto industry.**

- **While the two companies had the same intentions, their paths diverged when Toyota completed in-depth research with its target buyers, whereas Volkswagen started with a CEO-driven list of features, informed by little-to-no external input.**

- **What can we learn from both of these brands, and how do we avoid the mistakes of one and embrace the wins of the other?**

What distinguishes a luxury car from any other vehicle? Is it the price point? The look and feel of the car? Marketing and positioning? Or something else entirely?

Perhaps all of these factors play a role in making certain cars more prestigious than the rest — who's to say? Nevertheless, two car companies set out on a quest to make their marks in the luxury car space with drastically different results.

Toyota's Lexus stands out as a shining beacon of success. The Volkswagen Phaeton, on the other hand, made a splash for very different reasons. It's known as one of the greatest failures of modern automotive history.

Both companies had very similar goals from the outset. But over time, they made different choices and their paths diverged — leading to drastically different results.

What did Toyota do right, and where did Volkswagen fall short? Most importantly, what can we learn from their journeys to emulate one and avoid the mistakes of the other?

What fueled failure (and success)

In 2002, Volkswagen launched the Phaeton, the "pet project" of then-CEO Ferdinand Piëch. His steps to make this vision a reality were simple: He drew up a list of the features and functions he wanted the car to have, passed the list to his engineering staff and told them to make it happen.

Any marketer worth their salt will notice that a very important stakeholder group was missing from that process: the consumers who would (ostensibly) be *buying* the Phaeton.

When developing the Lexus, Toyota took a very different approach. The executive team sent engineers to Laguna Beach, California, and instructed them to consult with affluent customers and potential luxury car buyers. The engineers learned what these individuals' lives were like. Armed with that knowledge, they set off to create the Lexus.

It should come as no surprise which of these two cars succeeded with consumers. In his rush to create the next great luxury car, Piëch prioritized what *he* wanted to see over concrete knowledge of what luxury car buyers actually want. By eschewing market research, Volkswagen missed a crucial step that made all the difference.

Who's in the driver's seat?

In creating the Phaeton, Piëch took a confident step toward the car he was excited about. There's a fine line between confidence and arrogance, though.

Confidence *can* pay off. Industry leaders and game-changers like Steve Jobs essentially create new categories. But the Steve Jobses of the world tend to be one in a million — and luxury cars weren't exactly a new category when the Phaeton was in the works.

Absent feedback from the market, Piëch determined that he knew what was best. He thought he could create something better than the other cars out there, crossing into the territory of foolhardy arrogance. His approach ignored the intricacies of buyer perceptions and motivations toward the company's products.

What's more, Volkswagen failed to gather information about what consumers thought about the brand to begin with. Even if VW opted not to do market research specific to the Phaeton, understanding how consumers felt about the brand would have major benefits for the creation and rollout of the car.

If VW had done this research, perhaps Piëch and other leaders would have seen that people thought of the brand as "the people's car" — not a luxury brand. But the lack of upfront measurement meant that VW couldn't address this disconnect during the rollout of the Phaeton.

What made the difference between Piëch's way and the better way? One theory is his background. CEOs who have experience in customer-focused roles — including sales, marketing and product — are often quicker to consider what buyers want. And knowing how important consumer motivations are might drive more research and, ultimately, better decisions.

Keeping your mirrors adjusted

Buying a car is about much more than getting from Point A to Point B. Cars (particularly *luxury* vehicles) are status symbols. Drivers tend to view them as extensions of their personalities. For such a significant purchase, buyer motivations and the values they associate with a product are paramount.

When Toyota set out to create its luxury brand, the company's leadership grasped this concept. They knew that luxury car buyers look for a complete experience.

At great expense, Toyota created a separate dealer network for Lexus vehicles instead of selling Lexus cars alongside other Toyota cars. This branding distinction spoke volumes about the company's understanding of the luxury experience.

Volkswagen, however, sold the Phaeton with the same customer experience (and from the same lots) as its other vehicles. The luxury purchase process wasn't differentiated in any way. While VW did attempt to consider the customer experience at its Transparent Factory in Dresden, Germany (meant to showcase the manufacturing process), this effort wasn't enough to save the Phaeton.

Again, the clear distinction between these two brands was the result of Toyota's commitment to research-based and customer-focused decisions. Lexus continues to make strategic, thoughtful moves each step of the way. And those efforts paid dividends in establishing the luxury line in buyers' minds.

Turning the corner

The Phaeton isn't gone forever. The car found some success in China due to a customer segment that didn't quite exist in VW's other geographic markets: buyers who wanted luxury cars but didn't want to be showy about them. However, this quasi-victory is hardly the massive success Piëch foresaw with his dream car.

The Phaeton offers a cautionary tale to any executive who might reject market research in favor of their own way — and not just in the automotive industry. B2B brands that take an outside-in view of their strategy, talking to customers and embracing strategic marketing, *vastly* outperform competitors.

Rather than taking a narrow view focused solely on product performance, work to understand your brand's perception and the environment around you.

Those that choose to ignore customer perspective from the outset are left in the dust while strategic, buyer-focused brands like Lexus drive off into the sunset.

[Click here](#) or use the QR code below to go to an episode of the Accidental Marketer, where we discuss these two divergent paths, along with the problems and pitfalls that stem from an ill-informed top-down strategy.

Link to Accidental Marketer Podcast

A Tool to Measure Customer Perceptions: The Ability to Win

How do you work to understand customer perceptions — especially if your there are other factors besides performance that your customers care about (and there almost always are)? The Ability to Win (ATW) framework is perhaps our most powerful tool to do this.

The ATW brings together several outputs from previous steps (customer benefits sought, competitor identification) and adds some new data and information to help you understand the current perceptual reality of your customers. The analysis allows you to make changes to your offer before you launch or updates to your next-generation value proposition for existing products.

Ideally, you use market research to help identify the benefits as inputs and/or validate your benefits and analysis through the process.

The ATW looks complicated, but you will learn to use it immediately after you understand each input (NOTE: you might find it necessary to view the downloadable version of the Ability to Win tool in order to properly follow the instructions below):

How to Build an Ability to Win Analysis:

1. **For a target segment**, list the top 4-5 benefits sought that you identified in the Benefits Ladder Exercise.

2. **Weight** each benefit sought as the customer would, spreading 100 points across the benefits listed. The top ranked benefit sought from your segmentation analysis should have the most weight, with a declining balance of weight applied to the benefits customers would rate as lesser important.

3. **For each benefit sought**, list the two most essential critical capabilities that you can think of. Critical capabilities are assets and skills necessary to deliver on the customer benefit sought.

4. **Spread** the weight of each benefit across the two critical capabilities identified, according to the importance customers would place on each.

5. **Identify** the 2-3 most important competitors to measure your ATW against, referencing your Competitor Identification work. List your own company and these competitors across the top.

6. **On a 1-10 scale** ("1" means "couldn't be worse", "10" means "couldn't possibly be any better") rate yourself and your competitors based on *how your customers would do it* (not how you would) for each critical capability.

7. **Multiply** each rating times the critical capability weight and sum it all up. The result will be a total score for your offer and those of competitors.

8. **Analyze** the results — do they reflect the reality of the situation, or has your bias crept in?

[Click here](#) or use the QR code below to download an electronic version of the Ability to Win tool

Link to the Ability to Win tool

If you allow your bias to creep in, you might end up making the equivalent of a Phaeton! But if you complete your ATW with a reality mindset (including market research), you'll be able to make the changes necessary for success. Who knows, maybe your revised value proposition will be your industry's version of the Lexus.

Chapter 7.
How Can Smart Companies Bet On the Future — And Win?

Featured Case: Netflix

Tool: Differential Advantage

- **One entertainment brand has repeatedly predicted and adapted to key trends, from the rise of online shopping to the fall of VHS tapes to the streaming takeover. Netflix took calculated, forward-looking risks to secure its market share through major media evolutions.**

- **Through several stages of the company's growth, Netflix clearly mastered the discipline of predicting the future, responding to upcoming market trends and strategically investing in brave new ideas.**

- **How can businesses learn to see what's ahead, and what does it take to embark on an educated gamble of your own?**

Of course, nobody can accurately predict the future with any certainty, but some brands, more than others, have consistently demonstrated an ability to foresee what's on the horizon for their respective industries and adapt to emerging trends.

The minds behind one entertainment giant saw the writing on the wall time and time again: the trend towards internet shopping in the late 1990s. The beginning of the end of VHS — and the golden era of DVDs. The consumer's desire to rent rather than own. The shift away from TV as entertainment's focal point and toward other devices. The bandwidth increase that paved the way for streaming.

What innovator predicted and adapted to these many changes ahead of the game? It's Netflix, of course.

Netflix is a shining example of a business that took calculated, forward-looking risks through each stage of its growth. Their success in setting themselves apart from competitors and leading the way in entertainment innovation is impressive but not unattainable. As discussed on an episode of the Accidental Marketer podcast, other businesses can master similar strategies and practices to take their own educated gambles that drive market share. These insights show that, with the right approach, any company can emulate the Netflix effect.

How Netflix saw the future before others

Netflix's success story can be attributed to its ability to anticipate and leverage future trends in the entertainment industry. They have consistently been able to identify emerging technologies and consumer behaviour shifts and adapt their business model accordingly.

One of Netflix's earliest successes was recognizing the growth of internet shopping with Amazon and applying that same model to film rental. In 1999, they introduced a rent-by-mail service, which allowed customers to rent DVDs without the need to physically visit a rental store. This not only saved customers time but also provided Netflix with a massive database of customer preferences and behaviour, which they used to improve their recommendation algorithm and personalize their offerings.

As technology evolved, Netflix adapted by shifting from transactional to subscription-based models. In 2007, they launched their streaming service, which allowed customers to watch movies and TV shows over the Internet for a monthly fee. This provided greater convenience and flexibility for customers and allowed Netflix to expand their library of content without the need for physical distribution.

Netflix also invested heavily in their streaming technology, realizing that as bandwidth increased, streaming was becoming a better option than mailing out DVDs. This allowed them to provide high-quality video with minimal buffering times, and expanded their library of original content, which has become a hallmark of their service.

In response to the shift toward consuming entertainment on mobile devices, Netflix adapted its platform to be mobile-friendly. They developed an app allowing users to watch content on smartphones and tablets, adding another layer of convenience for customers.

By identifying shifts in technology and consumer behaviour, Netflix was able to adapt its business model and offerings to stay ahead of the competition. Their focus on innovation and customer convenience has allowed them to become a dominant force in the entertainment industry, with a presence in over 190 countries and more than 200 million subscribers worldwide.

Placing a bet: Predicting the future as a discipline

For the team behind any brand, foreseeing what's to come is more art than science — and it's one that Netflix mastered. But like skilling up in any field, getting better at predicting the future takes discipline: a regular habit of looking at what's coming around the corner.

Marketing teams need to engage in frequent and thoughtful discussions about potential trends, fostering an environment where innovative ideas can flourish. This regular collaboration can elevate the company's collective confidence in making bold, forward-looking decisions. For Netflix, this practice was instrumental in staying ahead of the evolving needs of both consumers and the market.

Forming this habit takes time, though — particularly when establishing trust with executive teams unaccustomed to taking forward-looking risks.

Senior leadership will likely not be won over after the first or second presentation of a trend-driven innovation, especially one that could change the course of the company. It might not be until the fourth, fifth or sixth presentation that bold, strategic moves — informed by careful consideration of future trends — gain traction.

Over time, as looking to the future becomes an essential practice and company leadership sees the value of taking calculated risks, innovative ideas will gain consensus.

Some companies that prioritize and practice innovation set aside a certain percentage — say, 10 to 20% — of their resources and efforts for trend-focused projects. These forward-looking explorations function like "planting seeds," and companies often need to give them time to germinate and grow before determining their success.

More often than not, those that see success with "out-there" ideas or pilot programs let the projects unfold, rather than killing them before they have a chance to work out early challenges.

Rolling the dice: Balancing risk and reward

While innovative company leaders must possess a willingness to take risks, they should see themselves not as gamblers making rash bets, but as bookmakers carefully calculating the odds and building a balanced book of risk and reward.

Unlike gamblers who may act impulsively, bookies take a big picture view of their potential gains or losses. They make informed decisions, shifting their assets as new information is revealed, and always having a stop-loss strategy in place. This is the approach that business innovators must adopt.

Instead of going all-in on a single opportunity, prudent innovators take a measured approach. They might start by dipping a toe in the water when they see a potential market opportunity, conducting further research, experimenting, or creating a minimum viable product to gauge the potential of an innovative idea.

The educated gamble is not about recklessness, it's about a disciplined assessment balanced with the courage to take the plunge when a trend-driven idea seems potentially transformational. Innovators must weigh what they might lose against what they could gain, taking courageous but calculated leaps that can pay off.

Companies' risk thresholds vary. Some leaders may seek what they consider "perfect" information and might not want to take a future-focused leap unless they feel close to 100% sure it will reap rewards. Others may be ready to move forward if they are just 51% sure an idea will work. Regardless of the threshold, the process of innovation is risky. The goal, however, should not be to eliminate all the risk but to gather enough information to make decisions that are more likely to succeed than fail. It's about making bets you can be reasonably confident in, not seeking perfection.

In the long run, companies that bet on future trends will experience the sting of failing on some occasions — that's the price they pay for taking risks that pay off.

Counting cards: The sweet spot of impact and probability

When looking at a future trend, forecasters within a company need to assess two things: the potential business impact of the trend and the probability of the trend occurring. For instance, Netflix had to consider how profitable DVDs would be if they eclipsed the VHS market *and* how likely DVDs were to take over.

While teams may reach a consensus on impact quite quickly, it's the probability piece that can be challenging to agree on. Trend forecasters may find, with repeated research, that lower probability trends — say, around 20% likelihood — are likely to have a major business impact.

Senior leadership needs to be repeatedly exposed to these patterns to understand the potential power of trends, even those that are less likely. Helping executives agree on the immense impact of the uncertain future further strengthens an organization's ability to innovate.

From there, it's time to prepare. Ready pilot programs or contingency plans that allow for agility if a simmering trend becomes more certain. This is another essential discipline of predicting the future.

Then, set up monitoring systems and "trip wires," such as metrics thresholds, that indicate it's time to throw resources behind a trend-driven innovation. (For Netflix, this threshold could have been, "If DVDs make up 10% of the market, we'll pivot to a DVD-focused approach.") Be sure that designated individuals at the company are tasked with watching the factors that could trigger those efforts — and take action when the stars align.

Winning big: Eyes on the prize

For those in charge of innovating and responding to the market, the discipline of the educated gamble is key. Stay attuned to the psychology of decision-makers and check-writers, and incorporate the right level of exposure to trends and risks to steer approval.

Predicting the future in order to drive innovation demands persistence and focus. But taking informed risks is the difference between the companies that stay comfortable where they are and the brands that make predictions and take gambles that pay off big.

Just ask Netflix: Stranger Things have happened.

Click here or use the QR code below to go to an episode of the Accidental Marketer podcast, where we discussed the strategies and practices innovators in any industry can master to take their own educated gambles that drive market share.

Link to Accidental Marketer Podcast

 **A Tool to Create a Differential Advantage**

A differential advantage is what sets your business apart from competitors and gives customers a reason to choose your products or services. To create a differential advantage, you can focus on three broad categories: employing similar tactics, changing the focus, and changing the rules. Netflix clearly went for the change-the-rules approach but for completeness here is a brief explanation of each approach.

1. **Employing** Similar Tactics

   To gain a differential advantage, you can utilize tactics that have proven successful for you and other businesses and simply do them better. Here's how:

   a. Study your competition: Research your competitors to identify the tactics they use to differentiate themselves. Look for patterns and analyze their strengths and weaknesses.

   b. Work closely with your customers to understand which aspects of your offer, and that of competitors, are most important to them. Identify those aspects that you can improve for maximum effect.

   c. Adapt successful tactics: Once you've identified the best practices, adapt them to your own business. Consider the unique aspects of your product or service and how these tactics can be tailored to suit your offering.

    d.   Continuously improve: Stay informed about industry trends and adjust your tactics as needed to maintain your differential advantage. Keep an eye on your competitors and be ready to adapt when they change their strategies.

2.   **Changing** the Focus

By changing the focus, you can emphasize unique aspects of your product or service that set you apart. You then increase the value the customer places on these aspects by promoting them against the current set of decision criteria. This is harder than simply doing it better but creates a longer-lasting advantage. Here's how to do it:

    a.   Identify those elements of your offer that you are particularly strong in when compared to your competition. Determine what makes your product or service different from the competition in the eyes of the customer.

    b.   Communicate these elements of your offer effectively: Craft a clear and concise message that highlights those elements you are relatively strong in. Contrast them to the existing priorities the customer has. Emphasise their importance while de-emphasising existing decision criteria. Make sure your marketing materials, website, and social media channels all convey this message consistently.

    c.   Deliver on your promises: Ensure that your business lives up to the claims made in your marketing efforts. By consistently meeting or exceeding customer expectations, you'll solidify your differential advantage.

3.   **Changing** the Rules

> To create a differential advantage, consider changing the rules of the game by disrupting industry norms. Here's how:
>
> a. Innovate: Develop new products, services, or business models that challenge the status quo. By offering something different, you can create new markets or redefine existing ones.
>
> b. Leverage technology: Use technology to improve efficiency, reduce costs, or enhance the customer experience. By doing so, you can set your business apart from competitors who are slower to adopt new technologies.
>
> c. Collaborate: Forge partnerships with other companies or organizations to create unique offerings or co-branded experiences. By combining resources and expertise, you can offer customers something they can't find elsewhere.

Click here or use the QR code below to download an electronic version of the Differential Advantage tool

Link to Differential Advantage tool

Chapter 8.
How Can You Build a Market AND Defend It As It Matures?

Featured Case: Viagra

Tools: Positioning/Branding

- **From the 1990s to 2017, erectile dysfunction medication Viagra and its parent company Pfizer enjoyed patent protection and market exclusivity. But Pfizer faces generic and low-cost competition following the expiration of its patent, as many pharmaceutical companies know all too well.**

- **Viagra put up a strong post-patent defense (starting even before it lost exclusivity) by segmenting its audience and building a still-market-leading brand.**

- **How can other businesses — pharmaceutical and B2B companies alike — face the loss of exclusivity to edge out their competition? What are the secrets to Viagra's success at becoming the customer choice in its category post-patent?**

For a business in its early days that enjoys patent protection and a complete corner on its market, life is good. The sun is out and the birds are singing. But when the dreaded day arrives and it loses exclusivity, all of that changes when tough competition from low-price solutions emerges.

In the 1990s, a Pfizer team developing a blood pressure medication discovered that it had an unintentional result for men: The drug was an effective treatment for erectile dysfunction (ED). Hence was born the medication we all now know as Viagra.

Until 2017, Viagra enjoyed patent protection that shielded it from competition. The drug averaged $800 million in annual sales, reaching over $1 billion in its early days. Parent company Pfizer had a formidable franchise in Viagra. But after its patent expired, the medication began facing generic competition.

Despite this major market change, Viagra still holds the number-one position in its category by far. Pfizer's market strategies allowed it to put up a strong post-patent defense against the competition and protect a significant portion of the revenue that Viagra generates.

For pharmaceutical companies and other industries facing low-price competition, Viagra offers a prime example of how to respond to life after exclusivity.

Building a brand and shaping a narrative

In retrospect, many of Viagra's brand-building strategies appear to have anticipated its eventual loss of exclusivity — whether they were or not.

When Viagra arrived on the scene, its market was a clean slate. The drug wasn't replacing or competing with another solution on the market, and it was treating a rarely discussed symptom to boot. As a result, the name Viagra became synonymous with the entire therapy area of treating ED.

The company invested in the strength of the Viagra brand for years before losing patent protection, and that work paid off: Viagra is, colloquially, the catch-all term for any solution in its arena. And the drug had built value in the brand itself, rather than just what it does.

Another aspect of its brand-building success is the nature of the problem Viagra solves — and the risk involved with switching to another solution.

For instance, if using a generic painkiller for a headache is unsuccessful, all the user deals with is a longer headache. But using a Viagra knockoff that fails when needed comes with a level of personal (and interpersonal) stress that most sufferers don't care to experience.

During its time of exclusivity, Viagra built customers' confidence that its product was effective — reinforcing that, in one's time of need, Viagra was the drug of choice.

Viagra promoted another narrative as well: the concept of ED as a spectrum. Viagra had to change the perception that needing ED medication was all or nothing: You either experienced catastrophic symptoms, or you didn't need the drug at all.

In reality, like many medical conditions, ED exists on a spectrum. By telling this story instead, Viagra came to be viewed as performance-enhancing, risk-removing and anxiety-reducing. This expanded the potential customer base by communicating that patients don't need to be acutely suffering from ED for Viagra to help them.

Low-cost alternative, high reward

Viagra made one other key decision which, while bold, substantially fueled the drug's success. Nearing the end of its exclusivity, Viagra released its own low-cost version of the medication.

This choice appears risky, particularly because drug companies can expect low-cost alternatives to take at least 20% of the market, as is the case with most generic options.

But Viagra's team looked at the impending market changes and thought, someone is going to get that generic business, and it might as well be us. The move strengthened the drug's overall platform and allowed it to continue to own the category.

Another stroke of brilliance came in releasing the alternative under a different name.

The low-cost version of Viagra was instead called Sildenafil, the name of the active ingredient in the drug. Because many people didn't know Pfizer released it, its brand equity remained intact. Viagra was still viewed as best-in-category, and the bold move didn't undo any of the brand-building work Pfizer had been doing for decades.

The need for discretion and the puzzle of anonymity

For businesses at every level of maturity, audience segmentation is an important part of go-to-market strategy. But it was particularly important for Viagra as the company considered what to do next in its lifecycle.

The sensitive and private nature of ED meant that much of the customer base for Viagra was deeply committed to discretion when purchasing the medication. Because of their hesitance to buy an ED drug at the pharmacy, many users purchased dangerous "Viagra-like" knockoffs online that contained shocking ingredients like concrete.

Viagra saw its audience's desire for discretion as an opportunity to take its own offerings online and sell the medication directly to customers through digital channels.

At a time when many other pharmaceutical companies didn't offer online channels, the risk of moving into the space was worthwhile for Pfizer. Offering digital, direct methods for customers to fill their prescriptions, Viagra meet the needs of the massive segment of its audience in search of privacy and confidentiality.

Pfizer found that, beyond picking up the prescription, many patients were hesitant to even speak to their doctors about ED. When Viagra was a billion-dollar drug, over half of patients experiencing ED didn't talk to their physicians about their symptoms.

The clear solution to this reticence was anonymity from start to finish. Early conversations about digital fulfillment questioned whether an ED diagnosis could occur without a doctor's visit.

But Pfizer showed determination to be a leader in finding safe, effective ways to remove personal interactions from the process. Pfizer struck a deal with consumer health startup Roman to streamline direct-to-consumer prescriptions of its company-owned generic: Customers answer health questions online, and a licensed physician reviews their responses then issues a prescription — no in-person appointment needed.

The company piloted fulfillment and shipping methods in several markets and worked with a specialized distributor to make the process as discreet as possible. Its efforts to met customer needs paid off, ensuring Viagra retained the top spot in its category.

From cornering the market to mastering the competition

In a competitive world, losing exclusivity can rock any company to its core. That's why at every stage of the business, the stronger a brand is, the better it will be able to withstand the changing tides.

If the end of your patent protection is on the horizon, plan ahead however you can, and don't be afraid of making the kinds of bold moves Viagra did in offering a low-cost version of your own product.

As risky as it may seem, rest in knowing that much of your audience values a known and trusted brand name, and their confidence in your product will continue to drive your success.

In the end, the lessons from this little blue pill just might be the cure-all for your loss-of-exclusivity woes.

Click here or use the QR code below to go to an episode of the Accidental Marketer podcast, where we explored what we can learn about bold strokes and brand-building from this little blue pill.

Link to Accidental Marketer Podcast

 **A Tool to Help Market Leaders Think Differently: The Positioning Statement**

Positioning statements guide the communication strategy of a brand. Marrket leaders in maturing markets refine their positioning statements over time to reflect their new prromise to customers, in light of new competitors or new circumstances. The step-by-step instructions to create a positioning statement — one that is unique, important and believable:

1. **Identify your target audience**: Identify the specific group of people you want to reach with your product or service. Consider need-based segments (based on values, attitudes, lifestyle). Use demographics (age, gender, income, education level, etc.) and firmographics (location, type of industry, size of company) to create a full persona.

2. **Asses customers' needs**: For each of the target audiences, what are the benefits that they seek, *or outcomes they are looking to achieve*, from any company (not just yours)? How might they answer "help me to….". Note that these are not features or functions — they are the types of solutions that they desire (e.g., no hassle, low/no risk, stay on the cutting edge, etc.).

   a. **Which of the benefits are most important to customers**. You may conduct market research, or have people who understand the customers help with this assessment (e.g., sales, customer support)

3. **Determine the positioning already owned by your competitors**: This is usually easiest to assess by using the Ability to Win (see chapter 6). Examine the benefits that are most important to the customers (from previous step). Find where competitors might already be strong and own a word or phase in your customers' mind. You may need to position against these perceptions.

4. **Determine your areas of strength:** Again, referring to the Ability to Win, what are benefits you can own in the customers' mind? Brainstorm a list with your team.
   a. Using the test — how <u>unique</u> and differentiated are you — relative to anything else available (including doing it themselves)?
   b. How <u>important</u> is the benefit to the customer? If the benefit isn't that important, your positioning won't resonate with them.
   c. How <u>believable</u> is your claim? Do you have evidence that can support your "owning" that benefit?

5. **Craft the positioning statement**: Based on the previous steps, create a concise statement that communicates your product or service's unique value to your target audience. It should be a single sentence that captures the essence of what you offer and why it matters to your customers. For example:
   • For [target audience], [product or service] is the only [unique benefit] that [addresses the problem/need].
   • [Product or service] delivers [unique benefit] to [target audience] who [need/problem].

> - Unlike [competitors], [product or service] [unique benefit] for [target audience] by [solving the problem/need].
>
> 6. **Test and refine the positioning statement:** Share the positioning statement with your team and get feedback. Does it accurately reflect your product or service's unique value? Is it compelling and memorable? Does it resonate with your target audience? Check again to see where competitors might already be strong and own a word or phase in your customers' mind. Revise the statement as needed until you have a clear and effective message.
>
> 7. **Use the positioning statement**: Once you have a final positioning statement, use it consistently across all your marketing communications. It should be incorporated into your website, social media, advertising, and other messaging to create a cohesive and memorable brand image.

Click here or use the QR code below to download an electronic version of the Positioning Statement tool

Link to Positioning Statement tool

Chapter 9

How Can Content Marketing Be Used To Build Customer Trust?

Featured Case: John Deere and the Case of the 19th Century Content Marketer

Tool: Content Marketing Guide

Key Takeaways

- **Long before brands built trust with customers in the digital sphere, John Deere paved the way for the future of marketing with its pioneering approach to communicating with its customers. In addition to having strong values and a solid reputation, the farming equipment company earned loyalty as perhaps the first brand to tap into the power of content marketing — as early as 1895.**

- **Instead of solely touting its products, John Deere focused on educating and helping its target audience of farmers through its monthly magazine, The Furrow.**

- **Why was this ahead-of-its-time approach so effective? And in a content marketing-fueled world, how can today's brands continue to stand out?**

When it comes to brand awareness, few companies boast the level of recognition of the farm equipment company behind a leaping stag logo and a yellow-and-green color scheme. For more than 180 years, John Deere has been making tractors for lawn and garden, construction, landscaping, forestry and more.

Throughout John Deere's tenure, plenty of notable traits have helped the company stand out. Its founder had a simple but powerful philosophy: *Treat everyone like you would like to be treated.* While many of today's brands today are still working to refine their mission and values, it's hard to compete with a straightforward stance like that.

John Deere was ahead of its' time in several respects, especially in its care for customers. To offset the high cost of its products, the company was one of the first businesses to offer a financing program for customers who wanted to purchase or rent equipment. But starting in the 1890s, John Deere was 100 years ahead of everyone else in another key tactic: content marketing.

Tilling the soil and adding value

In 1895, John Deere launched The Furrow, a publication about farming, for farmers — with the simple aim of offering advice and best practices to help them work more effectively. In today's ad-saturated world, it may seem too good to be true, but the magazine featured virtually no promotions for John Deere. *That's* content marketing at its best.

According to Oxford Languages, content marketing is defined as "the creation and sharing of materials that does not explicitly promote a brand but is intended to stimulate interest in its products or services."

Content marketing can educate, advise and even entertain the reader. Its effectiveness comes not from a company or brand promoting itself, but from providing value to its audience. As a result, the content puts the company in a positive light.

This was the case for John Deere. The Furrow greatly contributed to the company's success because, by helping its target market, the magazine secured farmers' loyalty to John Deere.

In today's noisy digital marketplace, everyone is a victim of over-communication — at virtually every moment of the day. So it's critical for marketers to give a would-be reader, watcher or listener a reason to tune in by offering them real value.

Simply telling your audience what your product does (and which colors are available) won't cut it. But if you can consistently capture attention with valuable and compelling content, you'll enhance your position in the market as you demonstrate expertise and even personality — just like John Deere.

Planting seeds and building trust

Beginning in the late 1990s, the power to unilaterally promote brands shifted from the hands of companies to customers. Rather than businesses simply telling the world what to think about them —- what become much more important was what customers thought of the product — *and* what they told others about it.

The arrival of the digital era meant that customers could engage in dialogue, not just with those geographically nearby but with like-minded others around the world. And the power of these relationships and recommendations made building trust with customers more important for companies than ever before. People trust *other people* — so the brands that built trust and loyalty with real people unlocked huge pockets of influence and, as a result, business.

Luckily, John Deere had a 100-year head start building this loyalty with customers through its content marketing. Rather than aiming to self-promote loudly enough to break through the noise (which can only go so far), the company proved its expertise *and* trustworthiness time and time again by educating its target audience.

The Furrow helped create customers for life. When trust became paramount to winning and keeping business, John Deere was poised to compete. For a century, the brand already had been setting itself up with an airtight reputation and a network of raving fans.

Fertilizing growth and driving demand

Beyond positioning itself as a clear market leader and establishing trust with audiences, John Deere's content marketing strategy brought additional prosperity. Because The Furrow focused on helping farmers do their jobs better, John Deere's target customers were able to expand their farms and businesses. With that growth came a greater demand for farming equipment — and having already built a relationship with readers, John Deere was a natural choice.

Tire manufacturer Michelin took a similar approach. By creating travel guides for the adventurous, Michelin built its brand as an insightful source, encouraging people to explore the wider world by car. Eventually, more road trips and miles traveled created the need for new tires. What better brand to choose than the one that publishes prestigious travel guides?

In both examples, the power of content marketing extends far beyond brand exposure or being seen as a potential supplier. Rather, the content (by inspiring its audience) embraces the opportunity to stimulate the market as a whole and to incentivize activities that ultimately lead to future purchases.

Some marketers may be concerned that this approach stimulates the market for their competitors as well. This is a valid risk.

However, when you inform and educate buyers in your product category, chances are they'll recognize your expertise as value that translates to delivering the best possible product.

Keeping customers' needs in mind will never let you down.

Reaping the harvest and reaching every audience

For B2B brands looking on, John Deere is a shining example of not only excellent content marketing but also effective audience segmentation.

When deciding what content will be valuable to create, consider the needs of each of the unique groups that buy from you. Get into the minds of different types of customers — their pain points, their questions and their day-to-day wins — and make content that addresses those concerns.

If you aim to self-promote, you'll struggle to gain attention. But if you aim to educate and help the people who buy your product, you'll gain their attention *and* their respect.

And you just might mow down the competition along the way.

Click here or use the QR code below to go to an episode of the Accidental Marketer podcast, where we explore what was (and is) so special about the agricultural ace that stands the test of time.

Link to Accidental Marketer Podcast

 **A Tool to Help Market Leaders Think Differently: Content Marketing Guide**

- **How to utilize the Content Marketing Guide**

A content marketing guide can help your company think through the specific ways that you are going to build trust with customers through providing helpful, unbiased and unbranded content. Creating a content marketing guide involves several steps:

1. Define your target audience: Determine who your target audience is and what they want from your content marketing. This will help you create content that resonates with them and meets their needs.

2. Set your goals: Identify what you want to achieve with your content marketing efforts. This could be increasing brand awareness, generating leads, improving customer engagement, or driving sales.

3. Conduct research: Gather information on your target audience, your competitors, and your industry. This will help you create content that stands out and addresses the needs of your audience.

4. Develop a content strategy: Create a plan for creating and publishing content that aligns with your goals and addresses the needs of your target audience. This should include the types of content you will create, how often you will publish, and the channels you will use to distribute your content.

5. Define your brand voice: Determine the tone and style of your content. This will help you create a consistent brand voice that resonates with your audience.

6. **Create** a content calendar: Plan out your content in advance, so you know what content to create and when to publish it.

7. **Create** your content: Produce high-quality, engaging content that aligns with your content strategy and brand voice.

8. **Promote** your content: Use various channels to promote your content, such as social media, email marketing, and paid advertising.

9. **Measure** and analyze your results: Monitor the performance of your content and analyze the data to determine what is working and what needs to be improved. Use this information to optimize your content marketing efforts and achieve your goals.

10. **Update** your guide: As you learn more about your audience and industry, update your content marketing guide to reflect any changes or new insights.

Click here or use the QR code below to download an electronic version of the Content Marketing tool

Link to the Content Marketing tool

Chapter 10.
How Can You Successfully Manage Your Business With Just A Few Metrics?

Featured Case: The Case of the Dubious Management Measure

Tool: Measurements and Reporting Tool

On a scale from 0 to 10, how likely would you be to recommend us to someone you know?" This question, forming the backbone of the Net Promoter Score (NPS), has been a measure for business success for nearly two decades. Though the NPS is a popular metric, it has limitations. This chapter examines NPS's strengths and weaknesses and discusses how Apple employs it alongside other strategies to drive growth.

Fred Reichheld of Bain & Company introduced NPS, which measures the likelihood of recommending a product based on an 11-point scale. Nine and 10 are golden, indicating high chances of continued business. However, NPS has been criticized for its simplicity and potential for manipulation.

Apple has been one of the most successful users of NPS in recent years. Let's take a closer look at how Apple uses NPS as part of its overall strategy and learn from its approach to maximizing the value of this metric. Apple has been using NPS since 2007 and is widely credited with getting it right.

1. Apple maintains checks and balances: To ensure the integrity of its NPS, Apple has implemented standardized data collection methods and consistently reviews customer feedback. By doing so, they maintain an accurate understanding of their customers' sentiments and prevent any attempts to game the system. Apple's commitment to maintaining the integrity of NPS highlights the importance of checks and balances in any metric-based system.

2. Apple speaks to a wide range of customers: Apple's success relies on its ability to cater to a diverse customer base. By gathering feedback from satisfied and dissatisfied customers alike,

Apple gains valuable insights into areas where they excel and those that need improvement. This comprehensive approach to customer feedback enables the company to make informed decisions that drive growth and innovation. The lesson here is clear: to make the most of NPS, businesses must engage with diverse customers and be open to positive and negative feedback.

3. Apple searches for the "why": While NPS provides a snapshot of customer satisfaction, it does not reveal the reasons behind the score. Recognizing this, Apple combines NPS with other metrics such as sales, revenue, and margins to create a comprehensive picture of its business performance. This helps the company identify the drivers behind trends and make necessary adjustments to their products and services. By digging deeper into the "why" behind NPS scores, businesses can better understand the factors influencing customer satisfaction and take appropriate action to improve.

4. Apple considers cultural differences: As a global brand, Apple recognizes that cultural differences can impact the way customers perceive and rate their products. By adapting their NPS goals and guidelines to account for these differences, Apple ensures that they maintain a clear understanding of customer satisfaction across diverse markets. This highlights the importance of adapting NPS strategies to suit the unique cultural contexts in which businesses operate.

NPS is a far from perfect measurement tool but when used appropriately and in conjunction with other metrics, it can provide valuable insights for businesses. Apple's case study demonstrates how a company can effectively use NPS to drive growth and improve customer satisfaction. By maintaining checks and balances, speaking to a diverse range of customers, searching for the "why" behind the score, and considering cultural differences, businesses can make the most of NPS and create a roadmap for future success.

Discover the do's and don'ts of this powerful but not infallible metric and how to optimize it for your brand.

Do maintain integrity — don't manipulate the score.

NPS's simplicity makes it easy to calculate, implement, and understand. However, this can also enable manipulation, especially when NPS affects stock prices. Any circumstance incentivizing high NPS — beyond genuine interest in understanding business performance — can compromise the score's accuracy. To keep NPS honest, establish checks and balances, such as randomly reviewing cases or standardizing data collection.

Do consult diverse customers — don't seek flattery.

When gauging business performance, avoid only consulting customers with positive feedback. NPS is meant to inform, not flatter. Collect data from a range of customers with honest feedback, including unhappy ones, to gain valuable insights and drive growth.

Do investigate the reasons — don't rely solely on NPS.

NPS is a leading metric, revealing trends before they occur. However, it doesn't explain the reasons behind trends. To understand business drivers, examine other metrics like sales, revenue, and margins along with NPS for a comprehensive view of performance.

Do account for cultural differences — don't treat NPS as a one-size-fits-all metric.

NPS may not be suitable for everyone, as cultural differences can affect scores. For instance, people in the UK or Asian cultures may be more reserved with praise. Businesses should adjust NPS goals and guidelines, accordingly, considering patterns over time.

Ultimately, NPS is meant to gauge the likelihood of recommendations. It's not an absolute metric, but one that should be thoughtfully adapted to best represent a business's growth goals.

Click here or use the QR code below to go to an episode of the Accidental Marketer, where we discuss NPS's nuances. Discover the do's and don'ts of this powerful but not infallible metric and how to optimize it for your brand.

Link to Accidental Marketer Podcast

 **A Tool to Balance Your Measurements: A Comprehensive Guide**

Our Measurements and Reporting tool will help you define a small but comprehensive set of metrics that will help you analyze your business. While the tool may seem intuitive at first glance it's crucial to apply it in a way that maximizes its benefits without overwhelming your administration capacity:

1. Prioritize Your Metrics: As a manager, it's essential to discern between those factors that warrant a metric and those that don't. Not every element needs quantification. Prioritize metrics for essential insights and feedback to avoid unnecessary administrative strain.

2. Begin with Leading Measures: Focus first on identifying the inputs crucial for accomplishing your business goal—these are your Leading measures. Assign a specific date to each of these inputs and decide on an optimal frequency — daily, weekly, monthly etc..

3. Transition to Lagging Metrics: Before diving into intermediate metrics, which can sometimes be ambiguous, shift your focus to lagging metrics. What are the specific outcomes you are trying to achieve, determine which metrics will validate success. How will you answer the question, "Did we fulfil our objective?" Bear in mind, lagging metrics evolve over a longer period and often align with standard business metrics like sales figures or market share.

4. Integrate Intermediate Metrics: Intermediate metrics bridge the gap between leading and lagging measures, providing insights into the project or campaign's trajectory. Consider the questions: "Are we on course?" and "Which metrics indicate our desired progression?" Tackling leading and lagging metrics first often equips project teams with the clarity needed to define these intermediate indicators.

> **5. Periodic Reviews and Retrospectives:** Consistently revisiting the Measurements and Reporting Tool offers a dual advantage. First, it prompts introspection—pondering on "How could this undertaking have been executed more efficiently or swiftly?" Second, it fosters a culture of continuous improvement, where lessons from past efforts inform and enhance future endeavours. After all, refining and optimizing is at the heart of any robust management methodology.

Click here or use the QR code to download an electronic version of the Measurements and Reporting tool.

Link to the Measurements and Reporting tool

By adopting this structured and balanced approach, not only do you streamline your measurement process, but you also position your future efforts for greater success and efficiency.